PIPEWO__
REVISITED
MORE PICTORIAL MEMORIES

REID PUBLISHING

Reid Publishing
53 Church Gate
Loughborough
Leicestershire
LE11 1UE

www.reidpublishing co.uk

reidpublishing@fsmail.net

First published May 2010
ISBN 978-0-9558807-3-5

Acknowledgements:
Written and compiled by David McVay
Typesetting and design by Tony Rose
Photographs courtesy of the Nottingham Evening Post
and the people of Nottingham who visited Pipewood Camp

Printed in Great Britain by the MPG Books Group, Bodmin and Kings Lynn

Mavis Lee (nee Savage) of Awsworth treasures these photographs of girls from the Coventry Road School, Bulwell class of 1947. She would love to hear from any of the girls, now ladies of course, among whom on the verandah are Ruth Tweddle, Dorothy Raynor, Pat Elliott, Mary Holden and Barbara Habgood

Introduction

ALMOST a decade ago, Patricia James of Carlton Hill in Nottingham wrote to her local newspaper with memories of a place called Pipewood.

She wasn't the only one. The mere mention of the word Pipewood was guaranteed to engender a flood of nostalgia.

Brian Cooper of Beeston Rylands is another Pipewood 'old boy' who felt compelled to place his memories on the record.

In the post-war years up until the early 1960s, thousands of Nottingham schoolchildren were whisked away from their homes in the working class heart of the city, to spend a month in the countryside.

Nottingham Education Committee had wisely identified the need to start rebuilding young lives after the deprivations of the Second World War and the austerity that followed.

They bought a former evacuees camp in Staffordshire and, with modest improvements, turned it into a haven for youngsters.

Patricia James eloquently and succinctly captured the essence of Pipewood when she wrote: "What a lovely time we all had, school in the mornings and scavenger hunts and quizzes and film shows in the afternoons as well as the large swimming pool.

"I remember every tea time we had large chunks of bread with strawberry jam. One day I broke one of my teeth and had to go into Rugeley in a teacher's car (which was a treat) to a dentist to have the tooth out.

Sunday was parents' visiting day and we had cheese and pickles on that day instead of jam. We used to like it when the butter machine went wrong and we

Continued over the page

had margarine a quarter of an inch thick.

"I was in Brackenhurst dormitory which we were told was haunted. The only haunting we saw was when one of the girls walked all the way down the room in her sleep.

"It was so good I went again the following year."

And Brian Cooper wrote: "I can remember Pipewood camp quite clearly and had some great times there for the princely sum of 24 shillings for the four weeks at a time stay.

"The main things I remember were that the boys seemed to get the better months of the year and the girls went later on, but no matter when we went the water in the outdoor swimming pool was nearly always freezing ... or so it seemed.

"There were four dormitories and the ones I remember are Hayend which I was in and the others were Heartsmere, Ravenswood and I think Brackenhurst, but not sure

about the last one.

"We used to get porridge and tapioca pudding (frogs spawn) but neither had sugar in and I think was probably made with water so most of us sent SOS messages home to 'please send sugar and jam if possible' to help sweeten them.

"It was at Pipewood that I first started smoking at the age of 11 and continued to do so until I was 22, but then realised if I packed up I could probably take Pauline and the kids to Ingoldmells for a holiday with the money I had saved by not smoking and this I

did and this encouraged me not to start smoking again, which I hope has helped to prolong my life.

"Another thing we did was to build a nest high up a tree in the woods which were part of the grounds. It was constructed of bracken sticks of which there was lots growing in the ground. We made it so big and strong that four of us could hide up there to have a smoke without getting caught, but one day Mr Cheeseman, who was either the head master or deputy head, saw us climbing up into the nest and ordered us all to come down.

"More out of fear than anything we just stayed there. He said he would wait as long as it took for us to come down and receive our punishment, but we stuck it out, and as it got dark he decided to give up, so we waited about 30 minutes and then climbed down and made a dash back to our dormitory and just hoped he hadn't been able to recognize us.

"We would walk to the

nearby town of Rugeley and buy anything that we could to sell and make a few pence on, and one time we caught a bus to Uttoxeter, which was about 12 miles away and got a telling off for being back late.

"On the third weekend parents and friends were allowed to visit and although this usually meant some goodies, sugar, sweets etc. being brought to help uplift our spirits, it was noticed that some of the kids who couldn't bear to be away from mummy and daddy any longer disappeared when the last buses were leaving, and the camp people seemed to accept it once they had made sure they had gone home and not just absconded somewhere.

"The teachers' names I can remember were, Mr Cheeseman, Mr Woolcott or Woolacott who was a teacher from Trent Bridge School; Mr Mitchell, Mr Ward, Miss Oats and Miss Dunne.

"We learned quite a lot about nature, visiting farms to help milk the cows. and swimming in the local stream/river down at Hampstead Ridgeware, playing shinty (hockey), football, tennis and going on cross country runs, which in my case meant running through someone's orchard on the route to gather a few apples to hopefully sell when I got back to camp.

"This was the best twenty four old shillings worth for a month's adventure anyone could possibly have had, and I have been back to the site a couple of times in the

later years when passing by the area, and spent a good 20 minutes or so sitting in my car and just trying to remember the good times."

Anyone who experienced the joys of Pipewood will draw something from Patricia's captivating nostalgia.

We have nothing like it today but, this is a different generation. Children have so much more to occupy their time, so many distractions and not all of them so healthy as a month spent in the Staffordshire countryside, giving themselves and their parents a refreshing break from the normal routine.

Today young children are just as likely to jet off to France or Italy with an expensive set of skis in the luggage hold.

Back in the 1940s and '50s, such luxuries were unheard of in working class Nottingham.

But that doesn't lessen the benefits of Pipewood

and who is to say that those post-war children enjoyed themselves any less than today's pampered teenagers?

From the memories that pour into our offices whenever Pipewood is mentioned, there can be no doubting the affect it had on so many young lives.

We wonder if, in 50 years time, there will be anything from the 21st Century that will remain in such a large, collective consciousness.

And so, due to phenomenal demand from the Pipewood generation, who responded to volume one by digging out more photographs to share with all those who made the journey, we are delighted to present a second collection of memories.

And perhaps this second book will prompt more of you to clear out the attic, scramble through boxes of old photographs and uncover a long-forgotten treasure of a magical time from your childhood.

The dining room in the summer of 1948 supplied by B. C. Ratcliffe of Borrowash, Derby

Pipewood Camp staff in 1954. Among those pictured, second left back row: Miss McNeil; second right back row, Miss Bates. Front row, from left: Miss Starr, Miss Synyer (later Mrs Chilvers), ?, Mrs Knight, headmistress; ?, ?, ?. Supplied by Mrs M K Chilvers of Nottingham

Ravenshaw House members from Haywood, Bentinck and Coventry Road schools. Also supplied by Mrs M K Chilvers

I went to Pipewood Camp for a month, believe the year to be 1958. I thoroughly enjoyed my time there, can remember choosing a nature class, going on walks through the wood, taking rubbings of the trees, collecting leaves etc. and then having lessons on camp writing about our nature trails.

The swimming pool was not in use and hadn't been for some considerable time. Looked forward to receiving the weekly parcels from home and the third weekend a visit from parents, where they were entertained by pupils.

We went to Rugeley every Saturday and visited Cannock Chase. The spending money we took with us was put in a school bank and we could draw this out when needed.

I have supplied five photographs *(printed left and on the following two pages)* taken during my time at the camp.

Hope you find them useful.

Carol Rollings
(nee Waller)
West Bridgford

Carol's group photograph

Carol Rolling's other photographs taken on camp. Left: Two taken on a nature trail. Above: Girls in their dormitory. Right: Head girl & boy with prefects.

The following four photographs have been loaned by Mrs D Lear (nee Ward), of Bulwell, who remembers submitting one of them to the Evening Post in 1996.

She writes: I could not believe the interest it stirred up. One (over the page) shows the dining hall in 1952. Notice the drinking mugs, no fancy cups then.

The teacher's name was Mr Dibbs. He took a lot of photos at camp, a bit of a Jimmy Edwards character.

The picture (right) shows the fancy dress party in 1952. Everyone had to take part, no excuses.

We had to parade on stage. I think for a lot of us that was the first time on stage.

We all clubbed together for bits and bobs to make them.

Continued over the page

The dormitory photographed in 2002

Continued from the previous page

The picture left, shows the netball and hockey teams. Cottesmore, Pierrepont Sneinton, Sycamore, just to name a few schools, all working together to enjoy themselves.

Again, we all had to play.

I hated games so I went to the camp nurse and said: "My thumb hurts. I think it's broken. I can't move it."

The nurse said: "So why are you moving it now?" She then promptly sent me out to play games.

Just look at the snow in the picture below. This was in March 1952. We are on our way to the dining hall. Gosh it was cold!

The dormitory was very cold, no double glazing and we all had to make our own beds, hospital corners, quite a mean feat when you are on the top bunk and not very tall.

We even had to take our vests off at night! Brrr! Yet, no one seemed to catch a cold.

I was a pupil at Farnborough School, Clifton and stayed at Pipewood in 1955, '56, and '57 in Ravenshaw and I loved every minute.

On one visit there was a mini flu epidemic and two of the huts were turned into hospital wards.

The final visit we all had to go home a week early as the boilers broke down.

What a shame as I left school that year

and never got another chance to stay.

I revisited in 1999 and the place hadn't changed except the verandahs were missing from the dormitories.

Mrs Patricia Bull (nee Bowles)
Nethergate, Nottingham

Above is a group of girls with their teachers supplied by Patricia

This picture of pupils from Trent Bridge School at Pipewood Camp in 1949 was sent **in by Bygones reader Barry Edwards, who lives at Winthorpe, near Skegness.** He said: "I was 12 at the time and I am on the third row from the top, sixth from the right.

"I am wearing a Boy's Brigade badge on my belt from the 9th Company. They were the days!

"I wondered if some of the boys would recognise themselves in the picture"?

Summer of 1948. Hartsmere Dormitory group photograph supplied by B. C. Ratcliffe of Borrowash, Derby

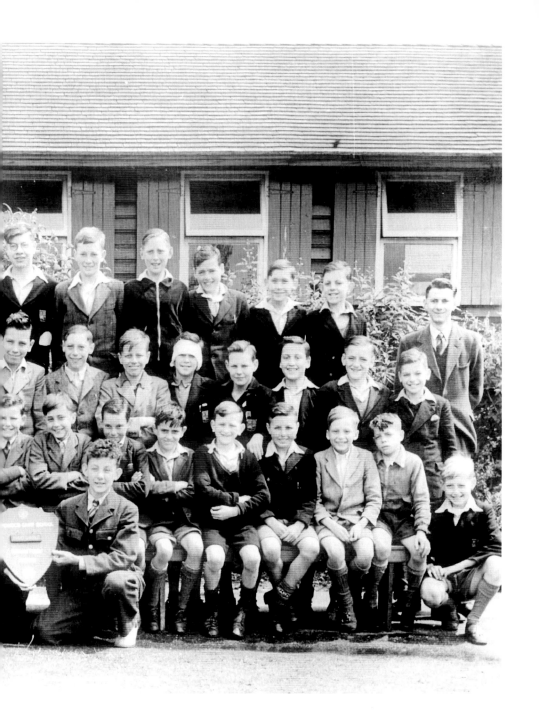

My sister Pat Butler and myself, Jean Butler, both went to Pipewood Camp two or three times.

It was really great, although I was homesick and couldn't wait for visitors' day to see mum and dad and receive some very nice chocolate cake.

We went to Trent Bridge School and we had a school reunion for 50 years at Boots Social Club ten years ago which was really nice. Some of the girls I hadn't seen since I left.

I remember very well going to Cannock Chase, Rugeley, for shopping, and Lichfield Cathedral.

Jean Pridmore
(nee Butler)
Chilwell

Two photographs supplied by Jean Pridmore

I visited Pipewood Camp several times with Cottesmore Girls School.

This picture is of our group from 1946. The two teachers standing together are Miss Dobson and Miss Pearson.

We had a great time — although on one occasion I caught the measles and was put into isolation.

We used to have midnight feasts from the parcels our families sent us. They weren't allowed to visit us until our last weekend there.

We went for three weeks at a time. I would love to hear from anyone who remembers me.

Pat Hutchinson (nee Dupuis) Gedling

Mary Cripwell of Ruddington suffered from Athletes Foot when she visited Pipewood as a pupil at Farnborough Road Secondary School, Clifton in 1955. She recalls:

"Previous to going I attended Chaucer Street Clinic (I'm sure many will remember this as a big rambling building) twice a week for treatment and eventually they said I could go providing I didn't use the swimming pool and wore something on my feet all the time. As it happened, when we got there the pool was closed."

Mary shared a dorm with girls from Cottesmore and Ravenshead and remembers her teacher Miss Smith (the lady in the lace top on the photograph) having a room on her own. She played a chopsticks ditty with her friend Ann Glew for one concert and sang She Wears Red Feathers and a Hool Hoola Skirt in another.

Names she recalls are Pamela Charlton, Jean Calcroft, Mary Tissington, Jackie Harrison, Jean Beecroft and Pat Freeman, who is standing next to Mary on the end of the right side. The photograph was sent to her from Pat Freeman.

Alan Aldred's brother Eric is mentioned in despatches in the Pipewood Papers magazine of September 1949 for winning the 'Senior Egg and Spoon Race' on Sports Day.

Alan recalls that at 24 shillings for a month, Pipewood was a bargain. Among his other photos are the William Crane school photo of 1949. Alan is pictured second from right on the front row and his brother eric is fourth from right on the back row.

Above: This undated group photograph was supplied by Trudy Loach (nee Betts) of Nottingham.
Trudy's husband is third from the right on the top row)

Right: An exterior view of the dining hall in 1946

Above: Pat Morley and Jaqueline Searle of William Crane Secondary Girls School at the camp in 1953.

**I went to Pipewood Camp
in 1951, 1952 and 1953
which cost 24 shillings
for four weeks.**

About 30 girls and one
teacher set off from Morley
School on the Wells Road
for this adventure.

We'd arrive at Pipewood

with girls from schools
around Nottingham.

We stayed in long
dormitories and slept on
bunk beds.

Every morning we were
up early to make a dash to
the ablutions block.

I don't think we had much

hot water.

We would make beds,
clean the dormitory and
ablutions inside and outside
every day before lessons.
Then the head teacher
would go around the camp
inspecting everything. We
would get marks on how

clean and tidy things were.

The dormitory with the most marks won the camp shield for a week.

Lessons were in the mornings and, after tea, afternoons were for all kinds of activities.

We'd write letters home and receive food parcels, then have midnight feasts, go to Rugeley on Saturdays, walk to church on Sundays and put on little shows. Families would visit on the third Sunday.

I could go on and on but I had a great time. I hope the girls from Morley Street recognise themselves in the photo, above.

Beryl Shurrock
(nee Shaw)
Nottingham

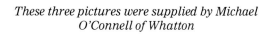
These three pictures were supplied by Michael O'Connell of Whatton

These two pictures (*above and over the page*) were taken in my last year at school.

We would go for four weeks at a cost of 24 shillings.

During my time at the camp we had trips to Rugeley shopping and nature walks to Donkey Hollow. Hands and shoes were inspected before going into the dining room and if not up to standard we had to

Shirley can be seen far left on the back row

run round the lawn in front of the dining room.

Each dormitory would put on a show and also a meal. They were happy times.

I went to Trent Bridge Secondary Girls School 1945-50. My maiden name was Fryer

Shirley Palmer
Netherfield

37

Preparing the table are Shirley Fryer, Marlene Weeks, Pauline Stevenson, June Barterelli, Thelma Tooms, Doreen Ensor, Joan Wood, Ann King, Shirley Atkin and Annette Snowdon
Picture from Shirley Palmer (nee Fryer)

I remember being at Pipewood Camp approx Easter 1957. I went to Guilford Girls Secondary School.

Whilst there we went to Litchfield Cathedral, and also to Dudley Zoo.

I was in the Maps and Plans classes (not my choice), but amazingly, I am still interested in the subject.

Mrs Mary Woods
(nee Walker)
Grantham
Lincs

Left from top left to bottom right: Mr Howard, Mr Bowlin, Mr Evans, Mr Joyce, Miss Abbott, Mr Pierce (Head), Mr Vingkman, Mr Davison, Miss Breedon, Miss Sim.

Below from top left to bottom right: Josephine Johnson, Iris Cutledge, Linda Fox, Carole Jolley, Carole Peet, Mary Walker, Gillian Beck, Susan Johnson, Christine Price, Doreen Stevenson, Sandra Yallop, Margaret Tyers, Joan Pallenter, Pat Hyatt, Hazel Trout, Margaret Helliwell.

The picture above was supplied by George Williams of Terrington St John, Wisbech. George is pictured top right.

Right and below: A visit to Pipewood Camp during the 1950s. Pictures supplied by Mrs P Brooks (nee Smith) of Sneinton

Keeping fit Pipewood style. Picture supplied by Pamela Vaile

I went to Trent Bridge School and I was 13 at the time. This group photograph was taken during my visit to Pipewood in 1945.

I am seventh on the back row, from the left. The one in front of me is June Reesby. Others I can name are Pamela Roper, Rita Chew, Doreen Green, Pamela Prince, Dorothy McKenzie. I know there were at least two Joans. Our teacher, to the right, was Miss Calvert.

I lived on Mayfield Grove, my name was Olive Taylor.

The other photo *(over the page)* is from the same school. We were doing The Snow Queen. I am the first on the left, sitting down. It was in 1946.

The one on the far end is Felicity Hudson. I know that she went to Tasmania.

By the way, I was a Buttercup.

Mrs Olive J Sheppard
Worksop

*Olive Sheppard's photo of a Pipewood production of The Snow Queen in 1946.
Olive is seated on the left*

I read with interest and lots of nostalgia the Pipewood Camp memories. I spent two summers there from 1949 to 1952 and loved everything about the camp, from making new friends, learning about the outdoors, the flora and fauna, hiking in the woods and just being away from the city of Nottingham.

I was a pupil at Bentinck Secondary School and the two group pictures show my classmates and me. The earlier one, *left* was, I think, taken around 1949 or 50. I am second from the right, 4th row up. My friend at the time was Sonia Dexter, 4th from the right on the same row. The second group picture, *below*, is from 1952 (the teachers signed the back of it). I am fifth from the left on row three and Sonia is tenth from the left also row three.

I remember her grandparents owned a fruit and vegetable store and we would all crowd around her when she got these wonderful food parcels from them. I lost touch over the years and often now wonder what became of her, as I

Continued over the page

Continued from the previous page

emigrated to Canada in 1968 and live in Toronto, Ontario.

My sister sent me the book and it has brought back so many memories, and I am glad I kept a few pictures of the happy times spent there.

On the picture by the pool, *above*, I am standing next to the girl seated who was also a friend, but I have forgotten her name. The pool was always so cold and full of leaves and debris, but we all went in, as that was something we never got to do much of in the city.

On the 3rd Sunday of our stay, it was Parents' Day, which was very exciting for us and we would put on some entertainment for them. Weather permitting there would be swimming contests and athletics and dance and also a play.

As I loved to ham it up I opted for the play. I am seated, picture opposite, but can't remember the play, except that obviously I played a male, judging by the moustache!

I remember the teachers, who were very jovial and not too strict, in particular Mr Dibbs, who was great fun. Going to an all-girls school it was the first time

we had instruction from a male teacher.

Things that come to mind are Friday lunch of fish and my favourite desert that day was always treacle pudding and custard. Saturday nights we had a social and had steaming mugs of cocoa and biscuits, what a treat when everything was rationed.

I hope you will find something of interest to help in your second edition of this wonderful trip down memory lane.

Barbara Hurling
(nee Wass)
264 O'Connor Drive
Ontario M4J 2T7
Canada

Sylvia Sheppard of Carlton was one of the first school children to attend Pipewood following the end of hostilities in the Second World War. Sylvia, then called Hawtin, was a pupil at Cottesmore Secondary School

Below: Still digging for victory from left are June Pritchett, Sylvia Hawtin, another, June Soles, Brenda Jones, Mary Earp, another, another, Audrey Norman, Pamela Dudley, Barbara Sykes and another.
Left; Wash day blues as Malvena Carthy, Elsie Jarvies, another, another, Sylvia Hawtin and Cynthia Charlesworth hang out the clothes to dry.

The Cottesmore class of 1946 sees Sylvia Sheppard on the back row, second from right

Sylvia Sheppard's Pipewood Camp group from October 1945 including Miss McNeal, cookery teacher. Sylvia is fourth from the left on the back row.

Right: You want MORE?!!! The dining room and anxious faces!

I attended Pipewood Camp in August 1945, probably one of the first groups to attend from Nottingham.

As a 14year old, who was a pupil at Trent Bridge School, I and others looked forward to our visit and stay at Pipewood. At that time my name was Joan Abell – now Campbell.

My recollection of the camp at that time was that there was no swimming pool, it may not have been operational for one reason or another.

As time goes by the memory of the Camp does not always recall all the incidents that took place, however, one of the incidents I recall was that rationing was still in place and we were given a small allocation of butter and margarine. I swapped my allocation of butter with another girl for her margarine, as she said she could not eat marg – (this is what I was led to believe!!). Was I conned?

It will be interesting to hear from any of the others who attended in August 45 (girls only at that time – no boys), and their recollections of the celebrations that took place when we heard that the Japanese had surrendered at the end of World War 2.

I recall that we were allowed to go for walks into the nearby countryside. One of these walks had a

lasting impression on me in more than ways than one, about nature in the countryside. I had the misfortune to sit on an anthill and got bitten by the little beggars!! Quite sore for some time afterwards – a lesson learned, always check where you intend to sit down.

Joan Campbell
(nee Abell)
16 St Andrews Drive
Uphall, West Lothian
Scotland

An unknown group of Chetwynd north girls pictured in 1952

Left: Joan Campbell (nee Abell) pictured on the steps of one of the huts. Do you know who took the photo and when? If so then please write to the address opposite

This set of signatures from April 1959 was supplied by Trevor Meredith of Tudor Court, Selston. Trevor attended Pipewood with fellow pupils from William Crane School

Opposite page: Sandra Jackson of Broxtowe Estate, Nottingham sent in this photo from 1960. Sandra is pictured left in the white dress and black cardigan.

Right: Pipewood Camp dormitory. Picture from Shirley Palmer of Netherfield

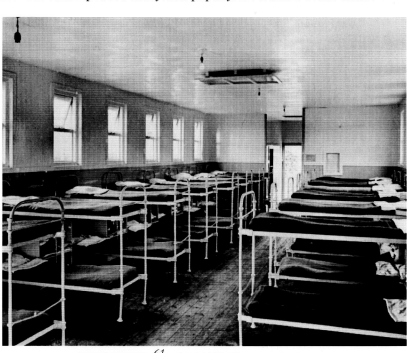

A good friend of mine sends me *Bygones* publication published by the *Evening Post* regularly and each one brings back fond memories of my early life in Nottingham.

Featured in the special edition No. 147 was a column on Pipewood Camp.

I was part of a group of children from Trent Bridge Secondary School together with other schools invited to enjoy a holiday in the late 1940s.

It was exciting and adventurous and unlike anything else experienced during the war period.

My father was serving in the Royal Air Force in India and my mother working in many jobs to keep the family going.

This picture is the only record I have. When looking at the individual faces I sometimes feel I know them,

but sadly not their names, except perhaps the boy on the back row extreme right, could be Michael Horne? I am standing next to him.

The teacher at the front was a very good singer. A sign of the time was the boy back row fourth from the left with a shaded eye-piece spectacles – the remedy for a lazy eye.

I hope this picture is useful in your forthcoming book.

Barrie W Roberts
Woodlands
Arnott Road
Holt
Norfolk

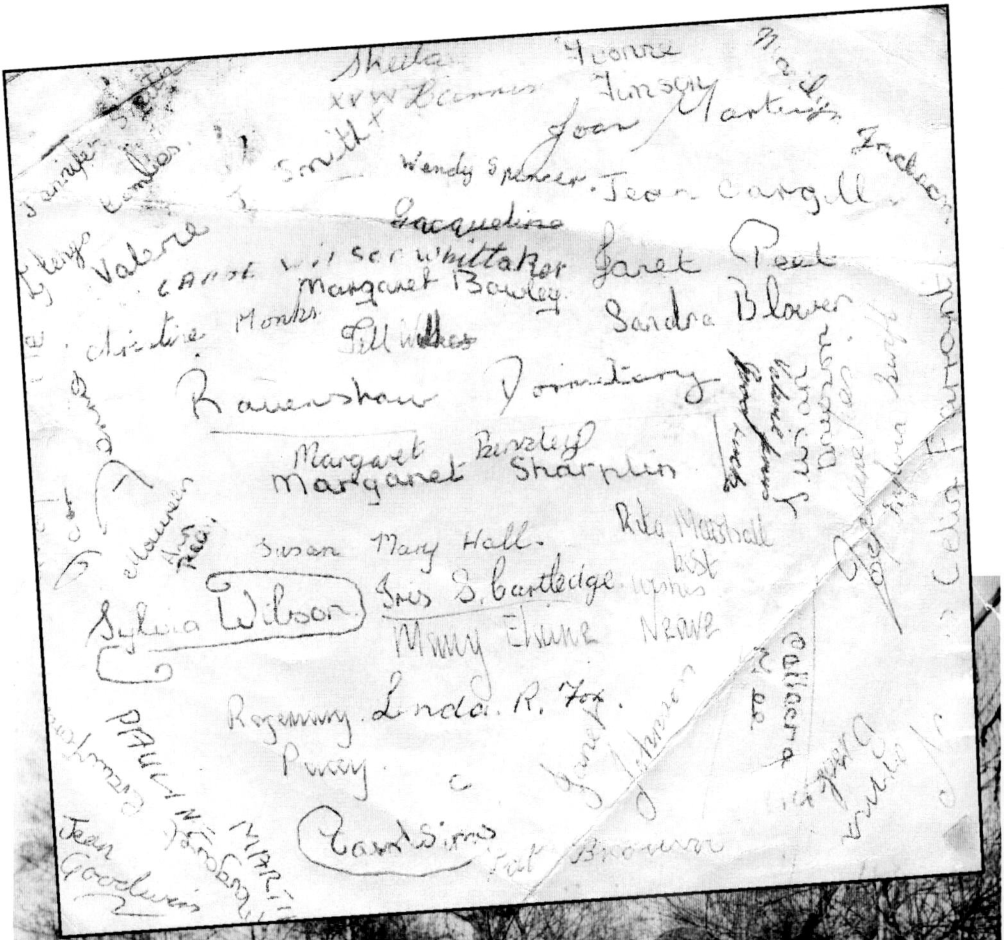
Ravenshaw Dormitory
Sheila
Jean Cargill
Janet Peat
Margaret Bowley
Sandra Blower
Wendy Spencer
Jacqueline
Whittaker
Christine Monks
Margaret Sharplin
Susan Mary Hall
Rita Marshall
Sylvia Wilson
Iris S. Cartledge
Mary Elaine Neave
Linda R. Fox
Carol Sims
Jean Goodwin
Brown

I went to Pipewood in the late Fifties, a wonderful experience. I was Joan Martin.

In the treasure hunt photograph, *opposite page*. I am the one on the right with school blazer, Margaret Glen-Bott.

I was in Ravenshaw North and made friends with Iris Cartledge and Norma Brooks.

We had to wash our hair on a Friday night to go to Rugeley Saturday morning, but my hair was always a mess after washing and because we would go to a coffee bar to see the boys I decided not to wash it and put a towel around my head. I just wet a bit at the front, but was discovered and made to go back to wash it.

My course at Pipewood was Pond Dipping, although I came without wellingtons, I had a great time.

The other photos show our group of girls and their signatures.

Joan S Brown
Melton Road
West Bridgford

This photograph was taken at Pipewood Camp about 1955. I am third from the right on top row. My lifelong friend Pat (nee Moore) is on my right and dear school friend Carole (nee Messom) is on my left. I remember many of the faces in the photograph but not the names.

Those days at Pipewood were indeed wonderful and memorable. Having just purchased your first edition of *Pipewood Camp*, I have been enthralled to recall those very happy days.

I recognise three of the faces on the front cover *(top picture)* – the blond girl sitting down on the left is Jean (nee Rogers) and the girl standing next to her, I think was called Margaret.

I stayed at Pipewood twice when both boys and girls were there together.

One thing I always remember was when saying grace in the dining room before meals we had to stand with our backs to the table (which sometimes when we had finished saying grace we would turn around to see that most of the bread had disappeared).

I don't remember anyone ever owning up to taking them but, boys will be boys!!!

I remember one trip to a nearby farm. I have always been a bit afraid of animals and the teacher was telling us where eggs came from. He was handling a hen and sensing that I was afraid, he took my hand and placed it firmly on the hen's body where the egg was formed and held it there for several minutes whilst he explained to the class all about eggs. It was quite traumatic for me but, of course, I came to no real harm.

I recognise several of the teachers but can only name two. On page 153 of the book *(top picture)* you show a group

of teachers, mostly names unknown.

The gentleman on the far right is Mr Pearce who was headmaster on both occasions when I visited Pipewood. On page 68 *(bottom picture)*, I believe that the lady third from the right on the back row was Miss Smith, who was in charge of our dormitory (Ravenswood South). We thought she was very strict at the time.

There are so many memories – midnight feasts, parcels from home, mint humbugs from the Bull and Specs (as we called it), climbing trees, country walks and so much more.

Thank you for bringing back so many wonderful memories edition.

Jean Kirk
Arnold, Nottingham

I think July 1945 was the first month the camp was open to schools from Nottingham.

My two pictures (here and over the page) were taken during that month.

I attended William Crane School, Aspley, and we shared a dormitory with Whitemoor and Bentinck schools.

No swimming pool then and very few lessons. Trips to Rugeley, Lichfield, Cannock Chase, etc.

A tuck shop to spend our sweet coupons in and, I think, a lovely month was had by all.

Jean Hackett
(nee Brock)
Bestwood Park

The second of Jean Hackett's photos taken in July 1945.

Two pictures supplied by Shirley Julian (nee Humberstone) of Haywood Secondary School girls at Pipewood Camp just after WW2. Shirley is standing on the extreme left in the picture below

I recently had the Pipewood book bought me for my 66th birthday which I enjoyed very much so I thought I would send you my photos of the time I was there, 1955-1957, I think.

My name is Lawrence "Lol" Milward. At school I was known as "Millie". I went to Berridge Road School, Nottingham. The mates I went to Pipewood with were Dave "Heno" Henshaw, Terry "Lol" Lawrence, and Robin "Rob" Holland. We

were in both Brackenhurst and Chetwynd.

We had great times there, not only learning, but having fun. We enjoyed the trips top Hampstall Ridware and Cannock Chase, where I saw my first snake, an adder.

In our leisure time we would go in the woods to build a den. When it was finished we would go and raid the other dens. We made a swing on one of the trees and everybody went on it.

The food was good but I didn't go much on the porridge. I haven't had any since. The tuck shop was the best and also the treats your Mum and Dad bought on their visits (3rd Sunday).

After we had shown them round the dorms and classrooms all the parents would go to the Bull & Specs for a pint and orange juice and crisps.

Very fond memories. Great days.

Lawrence
"Lol" Milward
Aspley
Nottingham

Teenager Nora Smith loved her months spent at Pipewood in the early 1950s.

Memories of the war were still fresh and after the grime and crowding of the old Meadows streets

where she lived, the open countryside and fresh air were a joy.

Now Mrs Nora Horton

of Wilford, she remembers those days with fondness and supplied this evocative photograph.

She was a pupil at Trent Bridge School at the time.

"It was open and fresh ... and the lessons weren't as hard as they were at school.

"And every Saturday we would go into Rugeley to spend our pocket money."

My name was Audrey Royston and I lived on Western Boulevard and went to Whitemoor Infants School and Guilford Girls Secondary Modern.

The two pictures *(below and the following page)* were taken when the girls from Guilford School went to Pipewood Camp.

This would have been about 1947. It was a very big thing for me as we went for a month and I had never been away from home before.

But I seem to remember I enjoyed it very much. Our families could come to visit us half-way through on the Saturday. My mum and brother Roy came but not my dad, he was away in the RAF.

We were members of the Guilford pipe band and we made the pipes ourselves from bamboo. I still have both of mine, a treble and an alto. Our music teacher was the lovely Miss Alvey who showed us how to make the pipes and we later went to the Lincoln Music Festival where, I believe, we came first in our class. The headmistress was Miss Lovatt.

Audrey Russell-Smith
Beeston

Looking back, most of my school days were during the 1940s, the war years. Some things I remember: The blackout, always having a torch handy, my mother always knitting and sewing as clothes were on coupons. She would always make a meal out of something. We never went without.

I had school dinners, a main course and a pudding for only 4d. Good value, even then.

We collected salvage on the way to school. I had my tonsils out at Chaucer Street and was in the City Hospital isolation ward for a month with scarlet fever.

When I came out they said I needed some sunshine, so I went to the Sun Ray Clinic on Parliament Street, near the big Co-op.

Then the war was over, everyone was pleased. We had made the best of everything. People had all pulled together, helped each other, no trouble then.

Then in September 1946, we were able to go to Pipewood

Camp for a month. The camp was in the Staffordshire countryside and the fresh country air would do us all good.

We went shopping at the nearby village — Hamstall Ridware — and to the church. It was harvest festival while we were there.

Trips to Tamworth and Lichfield cathedral, it was truly wonderful, a lovely time we will never forget.

All for £1.4s a month. I wonder if

our teacher, Miss Needham, is still alive, she is the one on the right of the picture.

I did go back five years ago for another look, it was then occupied by autistic children. Wonderful memories.

Mrs Willson's photo of Guilford Girls School, Basford, at Pipewood Camp in 1946

Mrs M. Willson
Valley Road
Nottingham

This photograph was taken at Pipewood Camp, when I attended Cottesmore Girls' School.

I spent one month there in 1948, and then again in 1949. I really enjoyed these times and we had such fun trips to Lichfield and Rugeley, walking through the woods at Pipewood and playing games. My name then was Margaret Ashwell and we lived with my Grandad at his shop at 190 Wollaton Road. I am in the middle of the front row; my best friend Avril Smith is second in from the right.

I cannot put names to most of the other faces, except for the twins, Mavis and Jean Fisk, not in my class, and one of the senior girls was called Gough, and we juniors thought she was pretty.

Like Mr Snowden, I too remember the winter of 1947. We didn't go to school at all, possibly because we had to go by bus. I do remember we sat the 11 plus

when we returned and that only the really clever ones passed (myself not one of these!).

A lot of us started school at Middleton School, Harrow Road, then on to Cottesmore. I worked at the GPO on Queen Street as a telegraphist. I married and my husband was in the Royal Air Force, then I was Margaret Smith. I divorced, married an American and became Margaret Hiller. As I was away from England for such a long time, I have lost touch with everyone. I would love to hear from anyone who cares to contact me: margaret.hiller@ btinternet. co.uk.

School friends: Phyllis Whitehurst (Hoult?); Janet Farnsworth; Avril Smith; Marian Davis (Kelvey?); or anyone else.

Work: Cecilia Thexton-Eunice (Dodds?); Chris Bateman (Meltam).

Mrs Margaret R Hiller
Thrapston

I stayed at Pipewood Camp for three successive years in 1954, '55 and '56.

On one occasion I was lucky enough to have my time there extended from one month to two months.

Unlike some who went home early I wanted to stay longer.

My older brother and sister, Brian and Margaret also stayed at Pipewood. But some years before I went.

I also visited another school similar to Pipewood in Derbyshire. I cannot recall the name of it. Maybe some former Pipewood campers reading this can.

Doug Roper
Walesby Crescent
Bilborough

Doug's photographs show (below) his younger brother Graham in short trousers. The larger image includes Doug, second row up fifth from the left wearing the white scarf. Graham is on the top row fifth from left.

I must say how much I enjoyed your first book *Pipewood Camp*. It brought back some wonderful memories I went to Cottesmore School, 1947-51.

I found three photos with me in the frame in that book. Also found some of my mates, Philip Cox, Lawrence Wryman.

I remember walking through Cannock Chase to the other side where a bus would pick us up and take us back to the camp.

I used to volunteer to clean the pool out on a Sunday, so I didn't have to go to church, keeping the dorms clean, just enjoying everything we did.

My two younger brothers also went to Pipewood Camp later on, their names were Douglas and Graham. I went a few times, once I stayed for two months.

I can say it was the happiest time of my young years. I shall never forget it ever.

Brian Roper
St Michaels Ave
Bilborough

The Second World War
had been over for just
a few weeks when June
Wright left her Radford
home to spend a month
in the countryside at
Pipewood Camp.

"I have read people say
it opened in 1946, but I left
school Easter '46 so it must
have been the summer of '45
when I went to Pipewood.

"I was seven when war
broke out and, as far as I
remember, we never went

anywhere for a holiday.
The beaches of course were
all wired off so there was
no chance of going to the
seaside," said June, who
lived in Schooner Street.
She is now Mrs Bailey and a
great grandmother living in
Arnold.

June was a pupil at
Radford Boulevard School
when she made her visit
to Pipewood. Some of the
friends on that same trip
included Mavis Robinson,

Iris Jones, Jean Newton,
Jean Brown and Audrey
West. "Unfortunately, the
photographs I had have gone
missing ... otherwise I could
have named all the girls,"
she said.

June remembers she was
in Brackenhurst dormitory,
shared with girls from the
Player School. "It was all
girls that first year, and boys
the year after.

"Our teacher was Miss
Waplington. We all had to

William Crane Secondary Modern School — Senior Boys at Pipewood Camp in 1949

behave in the dormitory because she was rather strict. You did not mess her about."

June remembers Pipewood being quite basic at that time, no swimming pool for instance, just a couple of lawns where they played.

"I remember we had a fancy dress parade. I went as a character from the Deep South. I blackened my face and hands with shoe polish ... it took ages to get clean."

And she recalls that Mavis Robinson won the chance to have her hair done. "She had a 'singer-wave'."

According to June, there was one major problem at that time. "Head lice were rampant in schoolchildren. Anyone found with the slightest hint was not allowed to go until they had been treated and completely cleared. Then they could follow on later."

Although it is now more than 60 years ago, June still has fond memories of Pipewood. "I can remember the camp fires with everyone gathered round, singing songs.

"Coming just after the war, it was just what we needed. I have never been back to Pipewood, but I have never forgotten those days."

Pipewood Camp, September 1945 or '46. Pictures sent in by Margaret Heath (nee Biddulph) of Gt Eastern Highway, Greenmount, Western Australia

This group of girls pictured in August 1947 was supplied by Mrs J G Greenwood of Wollaton

Unknown group of girls pose for the camera

This picture shows an entire group of Nottinghamshire girls in 1946. It was printed in the previous book but we felt it deserved to be included again — but much larger

In 1956 I went to Pipewood Camp with other girls from Sycamore Secondary School for a month.

When we arrived we had to stand in the playground until told which class we had to go to, I was in Ravenshaw Dormitory.

They were enjoyable days going to see different churches and then writing about the visits back at camp.

My friend Josie and I were asked if we would like to look after some little chicks which required us to dig for worms to feed them, I did not like worms (because they wriggled and tickled in the hand) so Josie collected them for the two of us.

I remember going to the tuck shop. We also used to get parcels from home in the post. One day we went on a bus to the local town to buy a present for my Mum and Dad.

On one of the Sundays my Mum, Dad, Aunty Marie, Uncle Wilf and cousin Pat came down from Nottingham for a day's visit. I have supplied a picture taken on the day, *below*. I am on the right of my Dad who is kneeling holding a young goat we had liberated from the stable behind us.

In 2008 my husband and I had a Sunday car trip to the Pipewood Camp and Rugeley.

It was a sad site to see it not in use.

Pearl Murfet (nee Stocks)
Bilborough

Above: Pipewood staff - date unknown

Right: A group of girls preparing for a game of rounders

I have enclosed two group photographs from either 1945 and 1949. I hope they might interest you.

The first one , *right*, was taken about September 1949 and has girls from Trent Bridge secondary school an Edale Road secondary school. The teacher on the right in the middle was Miss Hayward/Haywood. I am seated front row, fifth from right.

I do not remember very much about my time there, one memory that does remain with me is that we had to clean the swimming pool out before we could use it as it was full of frogs and debris. It was freezing cold most mornings.

The pool picture above shows me third left standing.

Porridge was served every morning and I remember writing and asking my mum to bring me some Golden Syrup when she visited as there was no sugar to put on it. I think rationing was still on.

The things I did enjoy were the walks around the countryside and going to the little church on Sundays, where the organ had to be pumped by hand. Those were the days!

Rosemary Wood
(nee Shippam
Woodborough

I have supplied two photos taken in 1952 on my second visit to Pipewood Camp, my first being in 1951.

The group photo (*below*) shows us with the trophy won for keeping the dormitory clean and tidy and many of the girls have written their names on the back of the picture. Not all the group were from Guildford School where I attended. I am on the back row fifth from the right next to Margaret Lacey, also a Guildford Girl.

The second photograph, (*over the page*) was taken when we had a fancy dress competition. My friend Jillian Hill is on the front row right wearing the old-fashioned bathing suit and I am next to teacher Mr Dibbs lookalike, wearing a new style bathing costume.

Although it is now 56 years since leaving Guildford, some of the 'Old Girls' still meet up including Jean Searle (pirate) and little Marjorie Bradford (Spanish lady) on her visits to see family and friends from her home in New Zealand, where she has lived for many years.

On the third Sunday during our stay at Pipewood parents were allowed to

visit and my uncle who had his own car brought my parents for a visit. It was lovely to see them, but sad when we had to wave them goodbye.

I enjoyed both my visits to Pipewood Camp, as there was always plenty to keep you occupied with visits to Rugeley on the Saturday, where you could buy presents for your family at Woolworth's and nature walks around the countryside. Sunday, we all walked to the local church, dodging frogs crossing in front of you as you did so. We were all encouraged to keep a diary, which we filled in during lesson in the schoolroom.

Just one thing I never liked and that was a dollop of fig paste with bread and butter for tea, as it never looked very appetising sat in the middle of your plate when you sat down to eat it.

I still have very fond memories of my visits to Pipewood Camp, and of the teachers that helped to make those visits so memorable.

Mrs Janet Hunter
(nee Clifford)
Hucknall
Nottingham

This photograph was taken of some of the girls who were in my dormitory at Pipewood. We were posing on the lawn in front of the Dining Hall.

After such a long time I have difficulty remembering all the names, but I give some of them below.

Some of them were from William Crane School but, of course, there may be a few discrepancies.

Back row L- R: Ena Leadbetter, Margaret Bartram, Barbara Pike, Brenda Peters,?, Christine Hughes, ?,?,?, Muriel Lyons, June Beresford, now Booth, Betty Johnson.

Front row L-R: Bernice Lee, Shirley Mellors, ?, perhaps Mavis Brown.

*June Booth
(nee Beresford)
Ilkeston*

Children watching the local hunt outside the The Bull and Specs pub. Picture from Mrs S. Fisher of Cinderhill

I accompanied girls from the Coventry Road Girls School in 1947 and again in 1948.

I was then known as Miss P S Bates.

My bedroom was at the end of a long dormitory, so we were on duty 24/7.

Formal lessons were in the mornings and afternoons were spent on recreational activities. On Sunday mornings there was a crocodile walk to church. Visits to Lichfield or Rugeley were a treat and much sought-after.

On one Sunday afternoon the girls were all dressed in their best as a coach load of visiting parents was expected. I urged the children to the windows to watch out, but was soon put straight by one wiser than me. "Nar Miss, they not come till the Bull and Specs as shut!" How right she was! As the coach departed we were short of one or two homesick girls. We were also left with a lot of clearing up to do, as baby sisters had been put down to sleep in the beds and crisp papers were strewn everywhere.

I returned home to find my boyfriend had married someone else on the rebound, and not one of the parents thought to thank me for giving up my own holiday to look after their children!

***Mrs Penelope Wells
(nee Bates)
Edwalton
Nottingham***

The following seven photos were supplied by Mrs Kay Burford (nee Woodhouse) of Gay Street, Huntingdale, Western Australia

Left: My first holiday at Pipewood, March 1957 In the recreation room, playing a game. I have a big black eye because my little friend with the plaits was swinging between two bunk beds, and I happened to be in the way. So I got a kick in the eye. Her name was Jill Marshall.

Right: Another picture from that year. Me front row, 2nd from right, and friend Jill Marshall, 3rd from right. Teacher Miss Smith (very strict) on left and Mrs Smith on right. Hope I have got her name right.

Another photo from Kay's first holiday at Pipewood. in 1957. Kay is on the front row, second from right, and friend Jill Marshall, third from right. Teacher Miss Smith on left and Mrs Smith on right.

Kay Burford's second holiday in June 1957 Some of the girls from Sycamore School. Kay is sitting on second bunk bed, second the from right.

This picture from Kay Burford shows an unknown group of boys and staff from June 1957

Kay Burford and friend Margaret Jones at Pipewood Camp in February 1960. Margaret is centre on front row and Kay is on her left

Right: In this classroom scene Kay's friend Margaret Jones is sitting on the back row to the right. Kay is next to her.

The picture above and the following three photographs of her husband Thomas's stay at Pipewood Camp were supplied by Mrs Margaret Linney of Hucknall. Thomas went to Claremont Secondary School, Hucknall Road.

The picture above shows Thomas relaxing by the pool.

Thomas Linney is on the second row from bottom left side wearing the plaid shirt.

Thomas Linney is on the back row, right hand side.

This photo from Mrs Margaret Linney shows boys hoping to be picked for a football match

Here is a picture taken at Pipewood in 1953. The majority of the boys are from Huntingdon Secondary School, with the rest made up from Manvers Street, both of Nottingham. Most of the boys on the back row were Gordon Homes boys, a home for local boys taken into care.

The other picture, *over the page*, would have been taken on the third Sunday of the month when parents visited. It looks like a relay race is in progress, at the

end of which, the boys would dive in for coins thrown into the pool.

I am in the group photo with seven boys from my class, 3A, of Huntingdon Street Secondary. Of the eight, seven met up this year with other boys for a reunion. We will all turn 70 this year so it will be time to celebrate.

M. McKenzie
Hucknall
Notts

*It looks like a relay race is in progress, at the end of which, the
boys would dive in for coins thrown into the pool.*

I was at Pipewood Camp in 1953 and clearly remember joining a queue to file past a television screen whilst the Coronation was in progress.

At the time I was at Cottesmore School and remember how, with two, or three, very close friends we were inseparable during the happy days there.

I have supplied six photographs from 1953.

**Janice Dodsley
(nee Pooley)
Beeston**

Opposite page: In the front of this trio is Judy Kinder followed by Janice and Sandra Onion.

Below: The girl on the left of this foursome is unknown but the other three are June Bagguley, Judy Kinder and Janice

Above: Top to bottom – Judy Kinder, Unknown, June Bagguley and Janice
Opposite page, top: Performance of 'Midsummer Night's Dream' (?) – Back left is June
Bagguley and Janice, side by side. Centre stage is Judy Kinder.
Opposite page bottom: Photo session at the farm – photographer Judy Kinder – subject
– June Bagguley, 4th from left in white blouse, Janice. Other girls unknown

Over the page: Ravenshaw Dormitory 1953 – Although June Bagguley and myself are clear
on the top row left and Sandra Onion is the fourth from the right on the third row from the
back with. Judy Kinder is immediately in front holding the Pipewood School Shield, the
rest of the group are unknown, but the majority were from different schools. Maybe readers
might recognise themselves

**I went to Pipewood for the first time
in 1947 when we had moved to live at
Sneinton Dale. (Edale Road School)**
I really did enjoy the times there.

Kate Bond
Long Eaton

Kate's photo of the recreation room in 1948

The recreation room in October 1947 supplied by Kate Bond

The pictures left and right were supplied by Mrs Barbara Stainforth of Burton Joyce, Nottingham.

Left: Four students from William Crane in 1951

Right: Two members of the teaching staff. Doreen Bond now Humphries is on the left. The other lady is unknown.

Far right: Four William Crane students ready for bed in 1951

Below is a group of girls from Cottesmore School taken in November 1946

Left: Jean Coffey's photo of the captains taken during one of three stays at Pipewood

Opposite page, top: Two pictures of teachers from the same period

Opposite page, below: Pupils from Player Secondary School for boys

Below: Jean Meakin (right), Valerie Hardy (centre) and a friend

I visited the camp three times in 1954, 1955 and 1957 and what wonderful memories I have of those times. They hold a very dear place in my teenage years.

I attended Player Secondary School for Girls and there would be pupils from other schools from Nottingham going to Pipewood the same weeks as us. Also Player Boys would go the same time as us and that is why I also got the photos of the boys 'dorms', as we would pal out with a lot of them.

Mrs Jean Coffey (nee Meakin)
Chapel St Leonards
Lincolnshire

Jean Coffey's photo of mainly Player School girls. Jean is on the second row from the bottom, fifth from the left

Another of Jean Coffey's photos of mainly Player School girls Jean is on the third row from the bottom, fifth from the left

My memories of going to Pipewood Camp at 13 years old in 1948, were especially of the outings we went on, to Cannock Chase, Rugeley and a place where they made pots, and being out and about in the countryside.

We had lessons in the morning and we were allowed to play most afternoons.

We slept in bunk beds which we made up every morning. I was with my friend from school, her name was Doreen Bishop. We all had a really nice time at the camp.

I would love to hear from any of my school friends.

Mrs Olive Ward
(nee Doyle)
97 Lindfield Road
Broxtowe
Nottingham
NG8 6HL
Tel no: 0115-9134332

Third row from the front: I am the sixth from the right, next to me is Sheila White, Doreen
Bishop, Rose Whitemoor, unknown, and Edna Barnes.
Second row from the front: second in from the left Ellen Goodman, Brenda Elnor, unknown,
Edna Barnes sister, unknown, then two teachers from Hartsmere 2.
The girls mentioned are from St Mary's School, Barker Gate, and Nottingham. The other
girls came from different schools

I spent a fabulous four week period at Pipewood Camp in the summer of 1949, whilst I was a pupil at Trent Bridge secondary School, Nottingham.

Although I did not have any photos taken during my spell at the camp, I have happy memories of life there – much of which has been described in the first book, e.g. farm visits, local country walks, exploring Cannock Chase, etc.

However there was an extraneous activity that was not on the curriculum and not mentioned in anyone else's reminiscences so far.

On occasional free afternoons, when no formal activities were timetabled, those of us lads who were keen on steam locomotive spotting would set off straight after lunch for a 40 minute walk down country lanes to Armitage railway station. This small station is situated on the West Coast main railway line and from a grassy embankment, which was an ideal viewing point overlooking the station platforms, we loco enthusiasts would watch the many main line expresses tearing through. Locos like the ex-LMS "Coronation Duchesses", the "Princess Royal's", the "Royal Scots" etc, were just not seen around Nottingham and seeing these massive steam

I remember having a great time at Pipewood, a wonderful month; I just did not want to go home.
It was a great experience and I remember my time there to this day. I was in the art class for most of the time, but remember doing the assault course, canoeing, and going to the local church on a Sunday morning.
I attended the William Sharp School in Bilborough.

Ann Fletcher (nee Breakspear)
Wrexham

Left: Ann Fletcher is fourth from the left and her friend, Gillian Daft, is fourth from the right, both on the second row down.

The exterior pictures above and top were taken in 2002

locomotives in action was a real treat!
It was always hard to tear ourselves away from this busy railway station in order to walk back to Pipewood Camp for our tea-time meal. We often ended up having to run in order not to miss it!

Ron Winfindale
Castle Ings
Spofforth
Harrogate
North Yorkshire

I was at Pipewood Camp in October/November 1947, the very bad winter.
A four week stay was extended to eight weeks due to an outbreak of scarlet fever. I loved the camp and had many happy memories.

Jean Rood
Arnold, Nottingham

This photo was supplied by Angela Szyszlak of Kimberley. Her father, Graham Cook, went to the camp with the Holgate School, Hucknall, in 1959. Graham Cook is on the back row in the middle, behind the boy in the check shirt who's sitting down.

I went to Huntingdon Street School, and I am very pleased to say that I went to Pipewood Camp three times, and enjoyed every visit.

On our second visit when we arrived at Pipewood we were told that we would be sharing our dormitory with some lads from Player School, everyone got on fine together. One lad comes to mind every time I start to talk about Pipewood, is a lad from Player who was a fantastic boxer. I think his first name was Patrick and pretty sure his surname was Kelly. He was fantastic to watch.

I have supplied a photo taken on the lawn, which

anyone would tell you, was sacred ground and no-one was ever permitted to walk on it.

Counting those sitting cross-legged as the first row. Third row, 6th from the right: Patrick Kelly, with black hair, open neck shirt. Keith is on the second row, fourth from the left, with white hanky in breast pocket. The year possibly 1947 or '48

Keith Carnill
Bestwood Park
Nottingham

These four photographs were supplied by Mrs J Andrew of
Hucknall who went to Pipewood in 1953.
Above are fancy dress prize winners from Guilford school.
Above right: A group of girls after a game of shinty which is
similar to hockey but with thinner sticks.
Below right: The Hayend girls with Miss Chew on the right.
Below: Girls outside during a geography lesson with Mr Dibbs.

Photo supplied by Mary Woods of Grantham. Do you recognise any of these faces?

William Crane pupils at Pipewood in 1954. Among those pictured are Rita Stone, Carol Boden, Georgina Moore, Sheila Stone, Maureen Palmer, Gillian Taylor, Daphne Saville, Valerie Bates, Janet Chambers. Photograph supplied by Gillian Walker

Little did I know that 40 years after spending a month at Pipewood Camp I would be living in Blithbury between the camp and the Bull and Specs pub!!!

I went to Pipewood in 1954 with my partner for the month Daphne Saville.

I had two Pipewood Revisited Reunions in the 1990's – lunch at the Bull and Specs, then on to the Camp, which had not outwardly changed, but had been modernised inside.

We have a 'Crane' re-union every year at the Park Tavern on Nuthall Road on the last Wednesday in March. Everyone is welcome both sexes and partners.

Gillian M Walker (nee Taylor)
Allington,
Grantham

Friends reunited in the 1990s. Pictured near the 'dreaded' swimming pool, are Christine Jackson, Pat Boultby, Carole Hind, Jean Wolfe and Janet Chambers. Photograph supplied by Gillian Walker,

Above: A reunion visit by William Crane ex-pupils to Pipewood Camp in 1999. This group are pictured outside the old canteen.
Below: Another photo supplied by Gillian showing girls outside the canteen in 1954.

A group of boys out on a nature trail. Date unknown.

A morris dancer is surrounded by Pipewood boys in the village of Hamstall Ridware in 1952

In our original publication *Pipewood Camp* we accredited photographs on pages 92-97 as belonging to Beryl Roulstone. In fact they were supplied by Jill Tulloch (nee Hawley) of Chilwell. We apologise for any error or upset and are happy to put the record straight.

Mrs Tulloch also points out that the unknown girl on page 18, in another of her treasured photographs, is Beryl Roulstone. Mrs Tulloch, known to her school friends as Jillian, adds:

My dad Frank Hawley was a councillor on the Education Committee at the time we were at Pipewood and came for a visit while we were there with the Mayor of Nottingham and other members of the council. We put a concert on for them. What fun.